NAVIGATING THE CONTINUING EDUCATION APPROVAL PROCESS

Dawn Fleming

An Infinite Wisdom Press Publication

i

Navigating the Continuing Education Approval Process

ISBN 978-0-578-03648-9

Infinite Wisdom Press, a division of
Energy Transformations, Inc.
1700 E. Butler Circle
Chandler, AZ 85225
U.S.A.

reikidawn@yahoo.com
http://www.energytransformations.org

Author
Dawn Fleming

Editors
William Fleming and Toni Neal

Technical Assistance
Amanda Sachs

Introduction

The information in this book is a rewrite of the book titled *Navigating the CEU Process*. Since publishing the original book in 2007, I was informed of the differences between the terms CEU and CE hour, which I explain in detail in the first chapter of this book. Like myself, for many years, most people have used the two terms, CEU and CE hour, interchangeably. A lot of people have not even heard of the term CE hour. What I have learned since writing the first book is that they are two separate entities. Therefore, I felt compelled to rewrite the book providing clarity, and additional information on working through the process as well as the changes that have occurred with the different approval boards since 2007.

The information in this book is geared toward holistic health and spiritually-related classes; however, the information can be used by anyone seeking to be a continuing education provider.

The journey of compiling this information as a book began when I was preparing a tip sheet for teachers who wanted to become continuing education providers. It then turned into a workshop, where I discuss these key points in-depth and offer my own experiences and stories along with some helpful advice for tackling this arduous process. The information that follows comes from over 12 years of experience, beginning in 1997 and working with over 10 professional accreditation boards (national and state level).

I began this process when many of the massage therapists and nurses taking my Reiki courses kept encouraging me to become a continuing education provider. The application sat on my desk for over six months before I engendered the courage to begin. I then set aside a couple of days to diligently work through the process. And that's how it all began.

When pursuing this path to become a provider, make sure that the classes that you want to offer to the various professionals directly relate towards the improvement, advancement, and extension of professional skills and knowledge of the respective career fields.

The information that I have provided is current as of the printing of the material; however, just be aware that requirements can change. I hope the information helps you decide whether you want to undertake this process, as well as assists and inspires you in navigating through this multifarious process.

Welcome to the world of Continuing Education!

Dawn Fleming

Holistic Health and Spiritual Educator

Director, Energy Transformations, Inc. and Infinite Wisdom Press

www.energytransformations.org

ACKNOWLEDGEMENTS

Many thanks to Carolyn Spinelli for recommending and encouraging me to become a continuing education provider. She was the catalyst for my first steps in applying to provide massage therapist CE hours. Thanks to Linda Roebuck for venturing with me through the first two CE applications. Doing this together made the process easier. Much gratitude to Toni Neal who lovingly provides her editing expertise. Thanks to my husband Bill Fleming for his love and support. You are a great cheerleader and editor.

CONTENTS

CHAPTER I

Understanding the World of Continuing Education

You are reading this book because you are a teacher and want to be able to provide continuing education credits to professionals that are interested in your holistic health or spiritually-related courses. You are probably unsure how this works or how many different approval authorities there are. You probably do not even know where to begin.

I began this journey in just the same place where you are right now. However, at that time there were no books on the subject to provide me guidance. When I began this venture, most of the information was not even available on the internet as it is today. I had to make a lot of telephone calls and ask questions of the professionals that wanted me to provide them continuing education credits. My success came from continual research to find who these mysterious approval authorities were, what they required, and how they wanted the information from me. I plodded along and learned a LOT in this journey of becoming approved by eight boards at the state and national levels.

I also learned afterward that not all professionals were interested in the classes that I was offering so I now keep my status current with only four of the boards. The information that follows is designed to make your exploration and application into the world of continuing education a lot easier than mine was. My best advice for you as you make the decision to become a provider is to be patient, take your time, be thorough, and be friendly with all the people that you deal with who put in long hours reviewing these application packets.

The term *continuing education* is a term that encompasses a broad spectrum of programs and post-secondary learning activities. Continuing education activities include degree credit programs, workforce training, formal personal-enrichment workshops, non-degree career training, self-directed courses, and experiential learning.

The term continuing education unit (CEU) and continuing education hour (CE hour) may seem to be interchangeable, but they are two distinct units for describing continuing education. One CEU is equivalent to 10 hours of class time; whereas, the CE hour is equivalent to one hour of class time. CEUs are what the colleges use to base credited classes on.

The International Association for Continuing Education and Training (IACET) is the caretaker of the CEU. IACET assumes responsibility for refining and disseminating information about the IACET CEU. Through its programs, publications, research, and technical assistance, the association assists organizations in correctly utilizing the criteria.

The CE hour is what is provided to most professionals that have educational requirements to maintain and uphold a license in their particular field of practice. These requirements are intended to encourage professionals to expand their knowledge base and skill sets, and stay up-to-date on new developments and techniques.

Depending on the field or profession, these CE hour requirements may be satisfied through college or university course work, courses offered by independent instructors or non-college schools, extension courses, internet or home study courses, conference, retreat or seminars attendance.

This book will address this category of continuing education, providing CE hours to those needing to keep their license/certifications current. You might have someone seeking CE hours mistakenly ask if you provide CEUs. The terms are used interchangeably by many; however, you now know the difference. It is important that you use the correct term, CE hour, when you address the various boards from whom you are requesting to become an approved provider.

In some career fields a CE hour might also be referred to as contact hours (holistic nurses) and professional development activity (PDA) points (acupuncture community).

This book will address courses that professionals are required to take after they have earned their degree or certification in their respective fields. The process that will be discussed in this book is everything that you need to know in order to work successfully through the application process to become a CE hour provider. This information will also help you to decide whether or not you want to begin the process.

In most cases, one hour of class time equals one point or hour. So when you are applying for approval to give these units make sure that you use the correct terminology and calculate the hours correctly. For simplicity's sake, I will refer to the units provided for this category of continuing education as CE hours.

Each board has its own approval process and criteria for providers and their courses. You must approach each board individually. My advice is to go through one process at a time or it could be overwhelming.

Some career fields have state boards that approve CE providers; some have national boards that are the only CE approval authority, while there are some fields where both the national and state boards approve CE providers.

If you find the latter situation, you want to ask yourself if you are going to teach your workshop in multiple states. If the answer is yes, go for approval from the national board. If the answer is no, start at the state level. Most of the time the state level has fewer requirements and their process is faster and less complicated.

CHAPTER 2

What are the Benefits of Becoming a CE Provider?

So you are going to go through all this paperwork and headache...why? Because you will attract more students to your classes. Your enrollment will increase provided that you advertise effectively.

I have been told by the professionals attending my classes for CE hour that they look for the holistic health classes for several reasons: they are tired of the same conventional style workshops that do not provide anything new; they can use the information in holistic classes for their personal well-being as well as for their professional use; and they see great value in holistic health-based approaches.

After you receive approval, this lends credibility to you and your programs or classes. This is because you have been acknowledged by a state or national professional board as a provider of professional level training.

This also opens possible opportunities for you to teach in hospitals, massage schools, acupuncture schools, community colleges and universities to professionals that need continuing education hours. A business that employs a lot of professionals may sponsor you to teach at their facility during off-hours so that their employees can get their required CE hours.

Professionals tend to spread the word to others in their field if they had a good experience. Referrals are free advertising.

You might be invited to speak at the respective boards' conferences or meetings. If you are not invited, ask the person who is in charge of planning the conference if you can be a presenter. Be proactive. Promote yourself. Receiving CE approval by the board makes opening the door to these types of organizations a bit easier.

You never know where the connections that you make through these boards may take you. Be open to the possibilities.

CHAPTER 3

Methods for Providing Continuing Education

The method of delivering CE hour courses can include traditional seminars, workshops, or classroom lectures with time allotted for practicing the information being taught. Distant learning or independent study is also an option in providing continuing education hours. Distant learning can be delivered in various forms: internet delivery, online interactive courses, teleconferences, home study, making use of books, CDs, and DVDs. It can be also offered as a combination of all of the above.

In addition to those methods already listed, you can also offer continuing education opportunities in conferences, conventions, and retreat settings.

As you can imagine, conferences and retreats offer more than just time spent learning or practicing techniques. A lot of time can be spent walking through vendor displays, sitting in meditation, resting, and sightseeing. In calculating the CE hours offered in these settings, only the time in which the participant is engaged in a learning activity counts toward the hours that can be provided. When you seek approval for a conference, convention or retreat, you will calculate the amount of CE hours that you are seeking based on the hours of the actual class time.

You will also have to have a sign-in sheet at each of the classes to ensure that the participants actually show up and attend the learning activity.

CHAPTER 4

What Boards Are Open to Holistic Health Workshops?

Examine what career fields in your state require CE hours. Not all states require that medical professionals and therapists comply with a CE requirement.

The national boards that are usually open to approving holistic health related classes are the American Holistic Nurses Association (AHNA), National Certification Board for Therapeutic Massage and Bodywork (NCBTMB), National Certification Commission for Acupuncture and Oriental Medicine (NCCAOM), National Association of Social Work

(NASW), as well as many state boards that are found under the state's Department of Health and Mental Hygiene or the like. Do not limit your search here. This is just a list of boards that I have worked with.

In the state of Maryland, I received approval to provide CE hours to occupational therapists and counselors. However, at the time when I received approval from them in the late 1990s there did not seem to be much interest from those professions in my classes. That said, things may have changed since then or maybe I did not find the right place to market my workshops.

Consider looking into the boards for emergency medical therapists, psychology, and physical therapy.

There is no national physical therapy board that approves CE providers. You will have to apply through your state board.

If you plan to teach just in your local area, you can look into the following state boards: nursing, physical therapy, counseling, occupational therapy, massage, acupuncture, psychology, social work, speech therapists, and/or emergency medical technicians.

Go online and look at your state's Department of Health and Mental Hygiene or its equivalent and see what career fields your course information relates to and research whether your state requires continuing education for those fields. There may be other fields that are not listed here that you can look into.

Be aware that some career fields do not have a continuing education requirement. After applying to AHNA and becoming approved, I found out that Maryland does not have a requirement for nurses to receive continuing education. Only the nurses that were specialized such as in oncology, psychiatric, etc. needed contact hours. This narrowed the number of nursing professionals that I could provide contact hours to in Maryland.

However, nurses in general are looking to learn more skills to integrate into their practices whether they need continuing education credits or not. Since I had AHNA approval for the classes, the nurses that did not need the CE hours also attended my classes because of the implied credential that AHNA approval provided.

When your class is approved by AHNA, since it is an accredited approver by the American Nurses Credentialing Center's Commission on Accreditation, you are allowed to offer CE hours to any nurse who might require continuing education.

CE hours for Chiropractors. When I asked the Federation of Chiropractic Licensing Boards (FCLB) about CE provider requirements they responded as follows: "There is no clearing house in chiropractic for CE courses. There is only the PACE program that the FCLB maintains for the credentialing of chiropractic institutions providing CE. If you are interested in obtaining CE approval for your courses, you would need to partner with an institution that provides CE in the state where you wish to provide your courses and develop an agreement with them to cosponsor your course."

I then visited the Maryland Board of Chiropractics website. The following information is listed on their site. "The Board accredits continuing education programs and courses based solely on their content. The Board insures that these programs are directly towards improvement, advancement, and extension of professional skills and knowledge in chiropractic. The Board may ONLY approve the credit of courses sponsored by a CCE accredited chiropractic college, the Maryland Board of Chiropractic Examiners, Maryland Board of Physicians, National Council on Chiropractic Education and Maryland Chiropractic Association or other recognized state chiropractic association. Independent courses conducted by contractors not affiliated/sanctioned by any of the foregoing will NOT be approved."

After reading this and visiting your chiropractic state board's website, if you wish to continue to become an approved provider, I would advise you to meet with the appropriate person at one of the local chiropractic schools and pursue accreditation for your class through the school.

Another fact that I learned from the Maryland Board of Chiropractics is that chiropractors can receive CE hours for teaching classes. "A chiropractor may receive up to 12 CE credits over the biennial period for teaching healthcare programs, classes or courses."

Visit each board's website (listed in the next section) and look at the workshops that have been approved. This will give you insight into whether the board is open to the subjects you are seeking to get approved. Even if it is not listed, do not stop there. When I began this process in the mid-1990s, there were not that many holistic health classes that had been approved in any field.

The following is the NCBTMB list of categories of courses that have been approved. Under each of these headings are a number of approved classes. Although your class(es) may be listed here, you still have to go through the approval process. Each person that applies has different credentials, teaching styles, and experience. The board needs to assess each person and their approach to teaching the information.

Animal massage

Aquatic massage

Aromatherapy

Body psychology

Bodywork – Asian studies

Business/marketing

Non-NCBTMB proprietary certification programs (e.g. craniosacral, myofascial release)

Chair massage

Deep tissue techniques

Energy work

Ethics

Health care massage (e.g., oncology, geriatric, pediatric, pregnancy)

Movement and exercise therapies (e.g., Alexander, Feldenkrais, stretching, Pilates, yoga)

Reflexology

Science (e.g., advanced courses in anatomy, physiology, kinesiology, pathology, above and beyond what is taught in a core curriculum program)

Self care (e.g., body mechanics, meditation)

Spa treatments

Sports massage

Therapeutic massage

Home study/Cognitive

Home study/Kinesthetic

Distant learning

Looking through the various programs that were approved, I was amazed and pleased at the classes the boards had approved. The various boards like certificate-type programs.

If you offer a course with over 30 hours, you can seek to have it recognized as an AHNA endorsed program. AHNA's endorsement provides your course more creditability and gets your course highlighted on AHNA's website. You do need to meet the requirements for being an endorsed course. These requirements include that the program has a scientific research base and that it is approved for contact hours by AHNA. In addition, recognized programs must teach knowledge and/or skills that can be legally integrated into nursing practice. Visit the AHNA website for more information.

The following is a list of courses approved by AHNA:

Reclaiming Astrology as a Relevant Tool for Holistic Nurses

The Art of Ascension

Aromatherapy

Meditation

Heal Your Past, Present and Future

Homeopathy

Group Empowerment Drumming

Reiki (all levels)

Quantum Touch

Equine Facilitated Integrative Healing

Energy Healing Training Course

Qigong

Herbalist classes

Spiritual Psychology training

An Introduction to Energy Healing

Certificate in Spirituality, Health, and Healing

Intuitive Powers Practical Application

Several types of Nutrition Courses

Body Talk Access Workshop

The Healing Power of the Labyrinth

Journey to Joy

Note the astrology class. Had it been written up as just an introduction course, it might not have been approved. However, this one that was approved was tailored toward the needs of nurses.

CHAPTER 5

Other Boards to Consider

When I went on the Maryland State's website and did a search on the words "continuing education," I was amazed at the number of careers that require CE hours. I offer the following list as possible places to explore if you believe your classes would benefit those professionals and that they would have an interest or see the value in taking your classes. Each state has their own regulations that govern the different career fields. Remember that some states require continuing education while others do not.

Dieticians

Emergency Medical Technicians

Audiologists and Speech-Language Pathologists

Vocational Rehabilitation

Counselors and therapists

Nurses

Occupational Therapists

Physical Therapists

Massage Therapists

Social Workers

Acupuncturists

Psychologists

Chiropractors

Teachers

A way to assess whether to pursue applying to a particular board is to observe what professionals are already attending your workshops. Ask yourself, what professionals might benefit from attending my classes, and what professionals do I have easy access to?

My involvement with becoming a CE provider expanded as certain groups of professionals began attending my workshops. Although I did have a number of laypeople attending, I would see trends forming. Do not pursue approval with a board where the professionals are not showing an interest. It is a waste of your time and money. Another category of continuing education is called Continuing Medical Education (CME) units. These units are approved by the Accreditation Council for Continuing Medical Education (ACCME). The ACCME's mission is the identification, development, and promotion of standards for quality CME utilized by physicians in their maintenance of competence and incorporation of new knowledge to improve quality medical care for patients and the communities. Visit www.accme.org.

There is a $500 per class pre-application fee just to see if the ACCME is interested in your class. The total process from beginning to end can cost up to $8,000 per class. This process is more challenging than applying for CE hour approval. From those whom I have spoken with that have completed this process, they actually had to have doctors and nurses help them work their way through the process. You need to make sure that you have the right credentials to teach physicians. You also need to be aware that you are required to send a video of your entire workshop to the board before they will approve it, or they will send two people to attend and access your workshop, at your expense. There is also a $2,000 annual fee to maintain your status as a CME provider.

Another group of professionals that you might consider providing continuing education is school teachers and counselors. This group is required by all states to pursue professional development. Each state has its own requirements. Classes such as meditation, stress reduction or emotional freedom techniques, might be approved; whereas, the more esoteric classes would not.

You will most likely need to check into the state's teachers requirements and get approval at the state level, and then apply to each county in which you are interested in teaching your workshop.

The National Board for Certified Counselors approves courses in the following content areas. If your class does not fall into one of these categories, call and talk to someone on the reviewing team to see if it is worth your time to apply for approval for that course.

Counseling Theory

Human Growth and Development

Social and Cultural Foundations

The Helping Relationship

Group Dynamics, Processing and Counseling

Lifestyle and Career Development

Appraisal of Individuals

Research and Evaluation

Professional Orientation

Multiple Sessions/Conferences ACA national conferences and a series of in-service sessions covering many topics.

Look into offering your approved courses at your local community colleges. Most community colleges have two categories of classes that they offer, credited and non-credited. The non-credited courses in a lot of cases offer CE hours.

CHAPTER 6

Where Do You Find the Boards?

Below is a list of the national websites to visit so that you can read over their requirements and download the required forms. If you are seeking approval from your state's board, visit that board's website and look for the appropriate information.

Since I have geared this book toward offering CE hours for holistic health and spiritually related information, there might be a category of professionals that I have not included to which you may want to offer CE hours. Go online and find that certification or licensing authority's website.

If someone in a particular career field asks if you provide CE hours and you do not at the time, ask them who or what authority you should contact to discuss offering them. Most professionals can provide you an organization's name or website that will lead you to the appropriate information for that field.

Websites and fees required for each board are subject to change, so check on-line for the current charges.

American Holistic Nurses Association, www.ahna.org. To apply for approval: email education@ahna.org. The cost for each course depends on how many CE hours you are seeking for your class. Renewal is every two years.

National Certification Board for Therapeutic Massage and Bodywork, http://www.ncbtmb.org, cost is $350 per organization or $180 per individual person. Both fees include all the classes that you submit. Renewal is every three years.

National Certification Commission for Acupuncture and Oriental Medicine, http://nccaom.org/diplomates/development.html, the cost is $50-$350 depending on what type of course you are seeking approval for. Renewal is every two years.

National Association of Social Work,
http://www.socialworkers.org/credentials/default.asp,
NASW has a one-time application fee of $110 for all first-
time providers. The price for each class varies depending on
the amount of courses you are seeking to get approved.
Renewal is yearly. I choose to get approval at the state level.

National Board for Certified Counselors,
http://www.nbcc.org/continuingEducation/providers/Appli
cation.aspx. Costs begin at $300 plus other fees do apply. I
have only dealt with the counselor's board at the state level.
It was much easier and less expensive.

CHAPTER 7

Getting Your Course Approved

What course should you choose to begin the process? If you teach a variety of courses, you might want to consider starting with a course that this particular board has already approved for someone else, such as a Reiki, Healing Touch or Meditation course. However, if you only teach one or two courses, start with the one that is easiest for you to describe.

You might have many different courses that you want to get approved by the various boards. Begin by seeking approval for courses that you have been teaching for a while. This way you have had time to work out any problems or issues and to get the timing down to how long each section takes to teach.

Calculating the amount of CE hours. In most cases one CE hour equals one hour of actual classroom instruction or practicum. Time taken for registration, travel, and meals cannot be counted in calculating the number of CE hours you are requesting. While many boards allow for a 10-minute break per each 60-minute interval, this breaks down to 50-minutes of teaching or practice and a 10-minute break with the total time counting for 1 CE hour. Get clarity for how each board calculates their timeframes before you start.

In most cases a board will not approve a class that you just developed if you do not already have provider status with them. This can be next to impossible if this is the first class that you are seeking to gain approved provider status. The boards want to know that what you are providing on the course description, learning outcomes, and time frames is how you are really presenting your course. This cannot be guaranteed with a new course. You will not know these factors to be true unless you have already taught the course.

The boards might even require that you send them copies of your evaluations providing proof that you have already taught the course and for them to see the remarks that the participants made.

A course that is taught in a classroom setting is a little bit easier to get approved because the instructor is present and can insure that the participant is fully meeting the course requirements.

For each course consider what questions someone might have about the subject that you are teaching. Make sure this information is included in what you are providing the boards.

In introducing new workshops that have not been approved before by a board, approach them with a positive attitude and word each learning objective so that it corresponds to that professional field's needs.

I do not suggest that you seek approval for classes that professional boards may consider inappropriate or *too out there* such as Wicca classes, ET classes, bi-locating, astral travel, etc. The information taught in the classes that you seek approval for needs to be relevant and the boards need to be able to easily distinguish its relevancy. The courses also need to meet the approval board's criteria as acceptable for their professionals. Review your titles and make sure they do not sound alarming.

Also make sure that anything that you submit to the boards is not alarming. You might think that your letterhead with dragons or angels is cute or that your *Hunting the Vampire* course is an irresistible must attend course. It might just be a turnoff to those reviewing your submissions. You do not want to miss the opportunity to have your (what the board would label) valid courses denied because of an *out there* or *marginal* course turned the board off to making you an approved provider. Do not submit wording or subject matter that might be too questionable. Make sure what you submit is concrete, clear, and understandable.

When you are submitting classes to the National Certification Commission for Acupuncture and Oriental Medicine for accreditation, make sure that the classes, and the wording that you use to describe them, are related to acupuncture and/or oriental medicine.

For each course make sure you have a good evaluation form that will meet the board's requirements. Every board will require that you have an evaluation form that you provide to their professionals after completing your course. You most likely will not have to mail them to the board, but you should have it on hand just in case they are requested. See evaluation form examples on pages 73-77.

Evaluation forms are very important because they provide the instructor with valuable feedback. If the instructor is really reading them, he/she can improve his/her courses or teaching styles, which will in turn improve the overall presentation of the course.

Once you have become an approved provider, it is usually easier to introduce new courses into the approval process. Each board handles this differently.

Distant learning courses or home study courses will require you to send a lot more information to substantiate the reasoning for creating the self-paced class versus a classroom version.

With distant learning and home study courses, you will be required to provide several sets of the materials that the participant would receive so that the continuing education reviewers can review the information. Make sure they look professional, and are clear and easy to understand. Make sure that any instructions are easy to follow and make sense. The boards need to feel that the information that you want to relay can be adequately taught in the format that you have chosen.

You will most likely be required to provide data from the results of a pilot group that worked through your course prior to application. This pilot group should consist of up to twelve people. Many of these participants should be in the professions that you plan to apply to provide CE hours. They should have already taken your proposed course and provided you feedback as well as kept track of how long each section of the course took to complete. They should also receive a copy of the test that you intend to give with the course.

You should provide the pilot group a lengthy questionnaire to elicit important factors that will help you to work out any issues and to make this an outstanding distant learning course. You will have to justify the amount of time that it takes to complete your self-paced course so your pilot group will need to provide you how long it took them to complete each section.

As stated in the previous paragraph you will have to include a copy of the assessment or test that the participants will be required to take in order to receive a certificate of completion.

Always work on providing the details for one course at a time. You would not want to put the wrong information on the wrong form and make the board think that you do not know what you are talking about or confuse them.

CHAPTER 8

Are Your Classes Appropriate for Their Professionals?

Just because you have your own credentials/certifications and offer workshops does not mean that each board will approve them. What are the names of your workshops? Are they too *esoteric* or *out there* or will the name of your workshop turn the board off?

Your workshops need to offer concrete information that the board will find relevant to their professionals. Give your workshops titles that do not make them questionable to the approving authorities. Make sure your course content supports the title.

You will be asked to provide a statement of purpose or description for each course. Make sure that your course purpose/description is stated in a way that is relevant to the career field that you are seeking to provide CE hours.

When you are looking at workshops to get approved, think of those that teach methods, processes and ethics; but also, consider getting approval for courses that are for the personal health and well-being of their professional.

You will be required to provide learning objectives/outcomes for each course. Learning objectives/outcomes, as they are referred to by the different boards, are a list of the knowledge base and skill set that the participants will possess after having completed your course. When you write the learning objective/outcome statements that describe your class use terminology related to that career. Use words that indicate that your class is appropriate for the professionals' career development. Also use one measureable action verb in each objective/outcome statement.

Each board has its own requirements on how many learning objectives/outcomes are needed per each hour of instruction.

They will expect enough information to be provided to support the timeframes that you are claiming for each objective. Some boards will request short bulleted statements that describe the content that will be covered to support your learning objectives/outcomes. This is the content section, which provides a description of the course content to be presented in sufficient detail to determine consistency with the objectives and time frames. The bullets should be short and concise similar to an outline format. For example, in getting my *Creating a Successful Holistic Health Practice* approved one of my learning objectives was:

Participants will market their practice.

The content that supported this objective was:

1. Paper Driven Marketing
   a.   business cards
   b.   flyers
   c.   brochures
   d.   articles
   e.   newsletter
   f.   mass mailing

2. Placing Advertisements
   a.   planning
   b.   cost
   c.   deadlines
   d.   research

3. Making your Advertisement Stand Out
   a.   color

b. words that instill action
c. stating what makes you unique

The stated time allowed for this learning objective is two hours.

As you can see there is enough information provided in this content to support two hours worth of teaching. You will also note that there are no verb statements in the content. The verb based statements go in your learning objectives.

Some boards have minimal time requirements (such as four hours) for workshops in order to provide CE hours. These requirements will be listed in the packet that they send you. Most packets are now sent to your email. In some cases you can go onto their website and download the forms and information yourself.

Do not take for granted that just because your class is approved for CE hours that everyone will sign up for them. The class should be relevant and useful to those in that career field. In order for them to attend the class, they must feel that taking it would benefit them professionally or personally, in addition to receiving CE hours. They may also look at your experience and qualifications before they decide to attend.

CHAPTER 9

What Should You Have Ready?

Each board will request a lot of information from you in order to determine whether or not to approve you as a continuing education provider. The information that the boards will ask for includes: a bio/resume, list of your certifications, examples of flyers, brochures, marketing materials, evaluation, etc.

Have an updated bio and/or resume ready. You will need to include this with any CE hour application form or you will need this information to include on the bio form that the board provides.

In your bio include a list of all the certifications and education that you have. If you are lacking in any of these areas, make sure that you emphasize any titles or related experience that you have. Also, be aware that with any certifications that you list in your bio, you may need to provide a copy of your certifications to the board. The reviewers need to feel confident that you are a professional and are qualified to teach their professionals.

Read the boards' qualifications carefully. The application process can be very time consuming and you do not want to begin without knowing whether or not you are qualified. I once applied to the Maryland state board to have a course for psychologists approved. They were looking for someone with a doctoral degree or some psychology organization to sponsor my class. Needless to say, my bachelor's degree along with my twenty years experience working in the field of integrative medicine was not enough. If they do not state an educational requirement, ask if they have one.
Look at all of the board's reporting, evaluation, and record-keeping requirements, and make sure that you are willing, and have the capability, to meet them.

Sometimes you can get an organization affiliated with a group of professionals to sponsor your workshop. You teach and they provide the CE hours. You most likely need to provide them your bio and learning outcome information. The school sponsoring you will provide you with any requirements that you will have to fulfill.

Have copies of the certificates that you provide to your students for each class you want to get approved. You will need to submit those to the board.

Have good outlines for each course that you want to get approved. You will use this information as part of your course description, and learning objectives/outcomes.

Have copies of your flyers, brochures, and marketing materials available. You will be asked to submit these also. They should look professional and be printed on good paper.

If you are not a nurse, but are seeking to provide contact hours for nurses through the AHNA, you will need a nurse planner to be involved in your program. This person will need to be involved in your planning process to ensure that what you are teaching is relevant to nurses and the training methods are professional and appropriate for the nursing career field. You will need to provide their name, bio, and contact information as part of your application.

For each class that you seek to provide CE hours, you will need to provide a copy of the certificate that the participant will receive upon completion of the course. Look at the example that the boards gives in its provider packet and make sure your certificate contains the information that the board deems important.

I provide participants with a course completion certificate based on the board's example and a continuing education transcript for the student. Below is an example of the transcript. The student gets a copy and I keep a computer copy for my records.

Energy Transformations, Inc
address
city, state, zipcode
phone number
Approved Provider #

Participant's name
Address
Phone numbers(s)
Email address
Instructor's name:

Course Title	Date Completed	CE Hours

Some boards may require a test and/or assessment be given to students to ensure that they understood what was taught. In the case of home study courses a test and/or assessment will be required.

Most boards require that you provide and collect evaluation forms. You might be required to provide a summary of the evaluations to the board. Use the evaluations to learn what areas need improvement and what areas you are excelling in.

Some boards may request an organization chart of your business. They are looking for who is the director, program administrator, instructor(s), treasurer, continuing education point of contact, etc.

Create a checklist of all the required materials that the board is requesting. Check them off as you put them together to send in your package. Some boards will provide a checklist with the approval packet. Make sure that you use it.

CHAPTER 10

Embracing the Process

If you have any questions about a particular board's process or forms, call them and get clarification. It is best to do it right the first time instead of guessing and have to redo the application. All of the people that I have spoken with on the various boards have been very friendly and helpful. In most cases an email can be sent to the approval board. Make sure that you do not annoy them with too many questions, particularly ones that can be answered by reading the packet of information that they sent you.

When you communicate with the boards, do so professionally. Make sure your emails are written with proper grammar and are to the point.

With some boards you might only get one try at making the right impression and documenting it the way they expect. Give it your best the first time. Most boards have a lot of applications to review, with very few reviewers to handle the load.

Good organization is important and will help you through this process.

Make sure anything that you submit is well-written. Have someone else review your whole package before you submit it. Make sure the forms are typed and not handwritten. Professional boards will not accept anything filled out by hand.

Before you begin to write, think about the professionals whom you are seeking to offer CE hours, and use relative wording such as, "teaching the *clinical applications...*". Think of wording that you can use that will relate how your methods or techniques can be integrated into that particular profession's field. It is important for the board to see how your class will benefit and relate to their professionals' career and personal needs.

Most boards will require that you submit learning objectives and teaching strategies. Teaching strategies are the methods that you are using to get your information across to the students such as lecture, discussion, demonstration, practice, etc.

If you have good outlines, you should be able to use a lot of this information and shift the wording to match the career field's needs with regard to what you are teaching.

Many professional boards can be very strict about the wording used on the forms. In your learning objectives, make sure you use just one verb in each statement.

When you are providing the information requested to describe the course, whether it is a title, course purpose, learning outcomes, or evaluations, think about how the reviewer is receiving your information. Think about whether this person, who has not taken your course, can understand what you plan to teach and the methods you plan to use. Your words and descriptions need to very clear and easily understood. Many people have different writing styles. Some are more easily understood than others. Do not be vague. Have someone that has not taken your course read over your application and provide you with feedback.

Learning objectives/outcomes seek to delineate the key points of information or skills that the students will be expected to know at the end of the workshop. The wording usually goes like this "Students will demonstrate..." or "Participants practice...." or "Students will examine..." and you fill in the blank with the different items that you are teaching. Some boards are more particular than others, so look at the examples offered on their website or in the package that you download.

Each board has preferences in how the information is presented – it is to your advantage to learn these quickly.

Learning outcomes must be stated in terms that are *measurable*. In effect, measurable terms are action terms, which use action verbs.

To quote the massage board application: "To understand the difference between measurable and non-measurable terms, let's take a look at an example. If during your course you review the muscles of the posterior neck and then show three techniques for stretching these muscles, two learning outcomes in non-measurable terms might be: *The participant will <u>learn</u> the 5 major muscles of the posterior neck*; and *The participant will <u>know</u> three stretching techniques for the posterior neck*. These learning outcomes are not measurable because it is not possible to measure what someone knows or has learned unless the participant demonstrates this knowledge in a measurable way.

These same learning outcomes stated in measurable terms might be: *The participant will be able to <u>list</u> the 5 major muscles/muscle groups of the posterior neck*; and *The participant will be able to <u>perform</u> three stretching techniques for the posterior neck.* The terms in these two learning outcomes that make them measurable are *list* and *perform.*"

When filling out the forms and describing the learning objectives use strong verbs such as those listed on the following pages. These lists are adapted from Bloom's Taxonomy for Educational Objectives and modified to reflect the verbs you would most likely use on your forms.

COGNITIVE VERBS include knowledge, understanding, critical thinking, synthesis.

KNOWLEDGE	*COMPREHENSION*
Cite	Compute
Count	Describe
Define	Discuss
Draw	Explain
List	Express
Name	Identify
Relate	Estimate
Repeat	Locate
Underline	Report
Tell	Restate
Translate	Review
Use	Schedule

APPLICATION	ANALYSIS
Apply	Analyze
Select	Appraise
Employ	Calculate
Categorize	Practice
Manage	Diagram
Question	Differentiate
Prescribe	Plan
Demonstrate	

SYNTHESIS	EVALUATION
Arrange	Assess
Compose	Compare
Construct	Create
Integrate	Evaluate
Manage	Judge
Record	Measure
Rate	Revise

AFFECTIVE VERBS include feelings, emotions, values, attitudes.

RECEIVING	RESPONDING
Accept	Behave
Attend	Complete
Develop	Comply
Realize	Cooperate
Receive	Discuss
Recognize	Examine
Reply	Observe

VALUING	ORGANIZATION
Accept	Discriminate
Balance	Display
Believe	Order
Influence	Organize

PSYCHOMOTOR VERBS perform a skill or activity.

PERCEPTION	SET
Distinguish	Adjust
Hear	Approach
See	Locate
Smell	Place
Taste	Position
Touch	Prepare

GUIDED RESPONSE	MECHANISM
Copy	Adjust
Determine	Build
Duplicate	Mix
Prepare	Set-up
Repeat	

COMPLEX	ADAPTATION
Coordinate	Adapt
Demonstrate	Build
Maintain	Develop
Operate	

When you provide your learning outcomes/objectives it is best to follow the flow of your class outline. Take each portion of your outline and summarize it into short learning objective statements using the active, measurable verbs listed in the preceding pages or any other ones that pertain to your teaching approaches and information.

Read over the instructions carefully on how the board wants your information formatted. You do not want to have to redo anything.

Start the process well in advance of the date of your class. Some reviewers can take up to four months to complete your review. For an extra fee, some boards offer to expedite the process.

When creating evaluations for the American Holistic Nurses Association ensure that the statements for rating the learning objectives on the evaluation match the wording used for the learning objectives on the documentation form.

Include a cover letter with the package. If you are already an approved provider with one board, make sure you mention that in your letter to the other boards. It will add credibility. Also, remember to enclose your payment.

Make yourself a copy of the package that you send to any board. It is always important to have a paper copy. Computers do break down and are replaced. Also, documents can be lost in the mail. When it comes time to renew, the paper copy will come in handy.

Once the board has received your package the information is given to several reviewers who will examine your information to ensure that it is complete and meets their criteria. If they have any questions, you will receive an email or telephone call. Do not get alarmed. Just respond promptly with the information that they are requesting. Just remember, they are trying to have enough information to be able to discern if your course meets their criteria. If you need the extra help, the AHNA offers tutoring for an hourly fee.

If you have not heard anything within four weeks, call or email the board and make sure they received the package. They should be able to give you an estimated completion date.

Upon approval the national boards will assign you a provider number. You will place this number on the participants' certificates and use this number when you correspond with that board.

Some boards have different categories for their continuing education programs. Make sure that you find out the category that your course is approved under. It might make a difference to the participants that need to get a certain amount of CE hours to fulfill the various requirements for each of the categories.

Have a generic certificate available. Some modalities just want proof of attendance and do not have an official CE application process. I have provided CE hours to Healing Touch practitioners and to aestheticians.

CHAPTER 11

Responsibilities After Approval

Once approved make sure that your contact and course information listed on the respective board's website is correct. Ensure it gets updated when your contact information changes; such as your web address, email address, home address or telephone number.

You should have a sign-in or attendance sheet for each class to ensure that those receiving the CE hours have attended. You should also collect the information that you will need for your database to track how many CE hours you gave, to whom, which classes they attended, and the dates of those classes.

Update and maintain your database of participants who received CE hours. Good record keeping is required by all boards.

If the class is multiple days, you should have a sign-in sheet for each day or take attendance to ensure that the participants getting CE hours are present for the time periods it is offered.

Make sure that you put the fact that you are a CE hour provider on your website and on all the flyers or advertisements for your workshops. Each board will most likely provide you wording that is acceptable to that board. Use it. Do not use the wording "CEU provider" on your website or flyers. Approval boards do not approve of this term and you might just be asked to remove the wording from your website.

The AHNA has a yearly requirement to report how many times you taught each class, the number of participants, the number of nurses, an overall evaluation of the class, and the addresses for each nurse and the number of contact hours that they received. Make sure you complete this form and send it in on time.

Most approval boards require that you reapply once every two or three years. Be aware of when you are required to renew your application. You most likely will not receive a reminder. Start a few months ahead of time. Do not forget and lose your approval status.

With the AHNA the renewal process requires that all programs and/or classes be resubmitted.

With the National Certification Board for Therapeutic Massage and Bodywork, once every three years you are required to fill out the application and only report the changes made to the classes or provide information on any courses that you have added.

Think about whether you can turn your classroom courses into home study and/or distant learning classes. Find out what the approval process is before you decide to go this route.

After receiving approval make sure that you teach in a professional manner. Most of the boards have a code of ethics and behavior that you are required to follow. The massage board listed some of the following as reasons to revoke their approval:
Unprofessional behavior.

Lack of boundaries between instructor and student.

Poor participant evaluations.

Sexual misconduct.

Improper dress.

CHAPTER 12

Marketing Your Workshop

Find the massage therapist organization American Massage Therapist Association (AMTA) chapter for your state and advertise in their local newsletter. Go to the local massage schools and leave flyers. Many community colleges now have massage programs.

Advertise in your state's NASW newsletter for social workers.

For other professionals, look for state newsletters to place your advertisement.

On your website, flyers, and brochures make sure that you note which career fields that you can offer CE hours.

See if you can offer free talks to the nurses, counselors, social workers, and therapists. This will let these professionals know that you exist and what you have to offer. Pique their interest and leave them wanting more.

Make sure that you have all of your marketing materials with you to hand out during or after the talks.

Have a sign-in sheet at the talks to collect email addresses and names to follow up with email reminders about your classes. You might even offer to send them a free ezine for signing up.

Offer to do a talk at a state or regional conference for the professionals that you seek to offer CE hours.

Make sure you have a website. Someone might not be able to make your current class, but may want to look up when your next class is offered. On your website indicate that you are a continuing education provider and name the fields for which you can provide CE hours.

Make sure the information on your website is current and clearly explains your class offerings.

Make sure that your website is registered with the different search engines and include the term continuing education or CE, along with the corresponding professional field names that you can offer hours to. You might want to use the term CEU in this case because a lot of the people searching use this term interchangeably with CE hour.

Use Google™ ad words to boost traffic to your site. It is a paid service. You will be able to put the term "continuing education provider or CEU" as part of your words to get traffic to your site.

Ask the professionals that you know in the field to spread the word. Referrals are free and wonderful. Ask them where you should advertise.

Visit your local schools that teach and certify the professionals that you are interested in teaching. Tell them that you are an approved CE hour provider. Inquire into teaching your classes in their school, see if they will let you leave flyers or if they will notify students about your class.

Visit the local places where these professionals work. Offer to give a lunchtime talk on your modality and then offer to teach your workshop on site during off-duty hours for their convenience.

CHAPTER 13

Putting It All Together

Now that you have taken in all the information, let's put this all together in a manageable "to do" list.

a. Identify the board that you are seeking approval from and get their continuing education provider package, either on-line or *snail* mail.

b. Read over the entire package before filling anything out and write down any questions that you might have or any thoughts that come to mind.

c. Do not handwrite your responses on the forms. Make sure everything is typed.

d. The information is usually sectioned into general/administrative: about you, your company and how you will handle record keeping of who has attended your classes and received CE hours; learning outcome forms for each class; and the documentation that supports your class as discussed in What You Should Have Ready.

e. Focus on filling out one section out at a time. Write down the areas that you skip and need to come back to or areas that require you to attach other information. You do not want to send in a form that is not complete.

f. Pay special attention to detail when filling out the learning outcome section. Be concise. Work on one class at a time. Make sure the timeframe for each element adds up to the total time taught (not including breaks and meals).

g. Put together or gather all the supporting materials: bio, evaluation, certificates, marketing materials, etc.

h. Assemble the whole package and have someone read through it. Make any changes and write a cover letter.

i. Make yourself a copy of the package as well as the number of copies that the board requires and enclose payment. Some boards still require that the package be mailed (not emailed) to them.

j. Begin the process again with the next board.

CHAPTER 14

Closing Remarks and Advice

You are the only one who can decide whether this process is worth the effort. When you fill in the forms, take breaks as needed. Do not get overwhelmed by the amount of information that you need to provide.

Only seek CE approval from one board at a time or you will become overwhelmed.

You are working with professional boards. Make sure all of your correspondence and interactions with the board members are done in a professional manner.

Make sure that you file a paper copy for yourself and save the last computer version of your submission where you will be able to find it in 2-3 years to aid you in resubmitting and/or updating your information for the boards. You will want to be able to find it easily.

Learn from each approval process that you undertake. The more boards that you decide to apply to, the more you will begin to familiarize yourself with the wording that is needed for other boards.

Maintain a high level of teaching standards so that holistic health classes continue to be sought after by the various professionals providing treatments and therapies to the mainstream.

Follow the standards of conduct and ethics that the boards require.

Hand out evaluations. Collect and read them. Make the appropriate changes to become a better teacher.

Be open-minded. You can always learn from each process and from the professionals that you teach. Listen to the words that they use to describe what they do. This will assist you through the application process and provide you the terminology used in that career field.

Your attitude will either support you through this process or sabotage your momentum. Work on the approval provider applications when you are in the right frame of mind that will support your completion and success. If you find yourself getting tired or frustrated, take a break and continue at another time.

Evaluation Examples

Below are a few examples of evaluation formats that you could consider using. Because of the small size of the pages the information's presentation may look a little bit unbalanced on the page.

Example 1

Continuing Education (CE) Workshop Evaluation Form

Name (optional): _____
Workshop Date: _____

Title of Workshop _____

☐ Check here if you do NOT want to be contacted regarding future courses offered.

Using the following numbers, please answer the following questions. If you would like, you may use the space provided for additional comments.

Question	5-Excellent	4-Very Good	3-Good	2-Fair	1-Poor	N/A
How would you rate the CE workshop overall?						
How would rate the instructor?						
Was there enough time provided for practicing the experiential parts of the class?						
How would you rate the quality of the handouts and manuals?						

Describe anything that you feel would improve this CE workshop.

Describe what was of value to you that was taught in this workshop.

Other comments

Some boards will require more in-depth evaluations that reflect the wording used in your learning objectives. Example 2 reflects a portion of a very detailed evaluation that I have used. The wording came directly from the course description/learning objective form.

Example 2

Participant Evaluation

Activity Title: Creating a Successful Holistic Health Practice

Date of Course Completion:

Purpose: The purpose of this program is to provide nurses the necessary information to begin or to expand a holistic health practice/business in a way that will create success, satisfaction and content clients that refer others to their practices.

Please rate the effectiveness of this continuing education activity.

5=Excellent   4=Very good   3=Good   2=Fair   1=Poor

Please rate the following:	5	4	3	2	1
Please rate how the class focused on the course objectives listed below					
Assess their readiness for a holistic health practice.					
Create a vision declaration					
Produce Goals					
Market their practice					
Identify their business needs					
Use the internet to promote business					
Networking					
Self care					
Please rate the overall quality of this class/training.					
Please rate how well the class was organized.					
Please rate the extent to which your expectations of this program were met.					
Please rate the overall quality of the materials provided.					
Please rate the following presenter(s):	5	4	3	2	1
Presenter Name: Please rate the instructor's expertise of the subject area.					
Please rate the appropriateness of the information provided.					
Please rate the Instructor's responsiveness to questions.					

Please describe new knowledge and skills you will apply in your practice learned from this activity.

Please describe how you may do things differently at work or with your clients after taking this class.

Would you recommend this class/workshop to others?

Did you feel the presentation was influenced by bias or a commercial interest? Yes____ No ____ If yes, please explain.

SURVEY

1. How did you hear about this class?

2. Why did you take this class/workshop?

Any further comments?

About the Author

Dawn Fleming has been working in the field of holistic health care since 1989 and teaching since 1992. Dawn is an Usui and Karuna Reiki® Master and intuitive healer and is the Director of Energy Transformations, Inc., which was established in 2004 to provide healing services and classes that empower and inspire health and well-being. Since 1989, she has studied Chakra Balancing, Therapeutic Touch, Cranial-Sacral Therapy, Usui, Reiki, Karuna Reiki®, Hypnotherapy, and Medical Intuition.

In 1994, she founded a non-profit, non-denominational spiritual center, the Beacon of Light Center, in which she held weekly meetings where spiritual discussions addressing healing were facilitated through the fall of 2004.

After receiving her Reiki Master certificate in 1996, Dawn began teaching all levels of Usui Reiki. In 1997, she received Karuna Reiki® Master certification from William Rand and now teaches all levels of Karuna Reiki®.

After studying and practicing various energy modalities, particularly Reiki, Dawn's intuition began deepening. She found that when she touched clients, their bodies provided lots of information on a variety of levels – physical, emotional, and mental. The journey continues to unfold for Dawn as she connects more deeply.

In 1997, Dawn received approval as a CE hour provider for massage therapists. She then began working on approval from various other national and state boards.

In 2003, Dawn developed and began teaching her own style of Medical Intuition. Geared toward holistic health practitioners who wanted access to more information about their clients during healing sessions, it allowed those skilled in the practice to provide more in-depth help. As a practitioner and teacher, Dawn is always learning and is in awe of the wonderful ways that healing has happened for her many friends and clients. She has taught classes at Anne Arundel Community College and Anne Arundel Medical Center.

Dawn has also written *Teaching Workshops Effectively* to provide guidance to teachers or to those planning to teach holistic health and spiritually related classes. Most teachers in this field do not have a degree in teaching. This book provides outstanding instruction for both the experienced and non-experienced teachers. Dawn also wrote the book *Creating a Successful Holistic Health Practice*. This book was written to answer the many questions that Dawn received from practitioners about her secrets to success in this field. This book addresses both the inner and outer work that it takes to create a successful practice.

For the left-brain world, Dawn has a Bachelor's degree in Business Management, has completed some work at the Masters level, and worked for 20 years in the federal government as a Senior Intelligence Analyst as well as a Senior Policy Officer. In November 2001, she followed her higher calling and resigned from her full-time job to expand the healing and teaching work, which was previously a part-time pursuit. Since 2001, her private practice has grown, as has the number of workshops and speaking opportunities she provides. The experience of developing and teaching many workshops, combined with her love of writing, led Dawn to develop this book as a great resource and guide for holistic health practitioners and educators.

Dawn's work promotes healing on all levels for individuals, groups, and the planet and empowers people to live happy, abundant, and healthy lives.

In this healing process, she wishes all her clients and students to remember their true nature, their unlimited potential, and their connectedness in Oneness with all

Creation and as co-creators with Heaven. In service to others, Dawn shares her knowledge through workshops and writing. To learn more about workshops that are currently being offered or to purchase other books or meditation CDs, visit www.energytransformations.org. Dawn can be emailed at reikidawn@yahoo.com

Many of the workshops that Dawn teaches are approved to provide CE hours/contact hours to acupuncturists, social workers, massage therapists and nurses.

Dawn Fleming is also available for speaking engagements, seminars and consulting/mentoring. For inquiries, you can email her at reikidawn@yahoo.com.

Books and CDs

Usui Reiki I and II manuals that Reiki Masters can copy and provide as manuals for their students without having to write their own or violate copyright laws. The manuals are designed so that they are easy to copy. These were written to provide a product that would be useful to all Reiki students and for those Masters teaching Reiki. Versions in English and Spanish. Cost for both manuals is a one-time fee of $49. Specify English or Spanish.

Creating a Successful Holistic Health Practice $19.95 This book provides valuable information on the inner and outer work to creating and expanding your holistic health practice into one that provides abundance and success. Ask about CE hours for taking it as a home study course. Purchase the CD *Meditations for Success* with this book and get both for $29.95 plus $6.00 shipping and handling.

Teaching Workshop Effectively $18.95 also available as an ebook for $14.95. This book was written to inspire teachers of holistic health and spiritual workshops to present outstanding workshops that motivate humanity to heal and inspire individuals and groups to explore their spiritual nature. In this book you will learn how to: prepare for your classes, market your classes, handle registration, price your workshops, and establish rapport. Many teaching methods are explored along with how these methods create student retention of the material. You will also learn how to handle interruptions, questions, and the "teachable moment."

Perspectives on Ascension: Sustenance for Humanity's Journey Home – $16.95. Thirteen writers provide wisdom for walking the path of awakening. Mixed with humor, poetry, and valuable guidance for today's world, this book is a must read for anyone on a spiritual path.

Meditations for Success $15. This CD includes four meditation exercises that align you with your vision of success and opens you to the abundance and success that is divinely yours.

Becoming A CE Provider – a 2-CD set of the workshop recorded live $25.00. Two and half hours of information that supports the information in this book. Dawn shares her experiences with the different boards.

Home Study Courses

Energy Transformations Inc. offers two home study courses that provide CE hours to both massage therapists and nurses.

Creating a Successful Holistic Health Practice - In this home study course you will learn how to begin a successful holistic health practice as well as expand a current practice. This workshop focuses on both the inner and outer work to create success and abundance. The manual has chapters on: treating your practice like a business, effective marketing, marketing materials, creating a talk, mastermind groups, networking, creating your vision, getting return clients, establishing rapport, showing your clients that you appreciate them, referrals, and much, much, more.

Chakra Wisdom – 24 Days of Transformation - Chakra Wisdom is about empowering you to release blocks in all areas of your life, to make the necessary changes, to heal, and to align you to create the life that you want. In doing so, you can assist your clients in their transformation processes. This course will teach you how to create a healthy, vibrant, energy field - essential to your health and well-being. You will explore the dynamics of the energy field, the chakras, and activities that you can do to maintain balance and vitality, along with exercises for you to do each day to strengthen your energy field.

Learn more or register for either class at
http://www.energytransformations.org

Products may be purchased online at www.energytransformations.org or at www.lulu.com or using the following order form

Please send me the following CDs or books.

_____

_____

_____

_____

Name:_____

Address_____

City:_____State: _____

Zip: _____Telephone_____

Email address:

_____

Sales tax for all purchases in AZ add 6.3%_____

Shipping: $6.50 for first book or $3.50 for first CD and $2.00 for each additional product.

Make checks payable to Energy Transformations Inc.

Total enclosed: _____

Energy Transformations Inc.,
1700 E. Butler Circle, Chandler, AZ 85225
You can also place your order online at
http://www.energytransformations.org

CPSIA information can be obtained at www.ICGtesting.com
Printed in the USA
BVOW08s0946060214

344024BV00002B/572/P